Dimetrodon

Written by Rupert Oliver
Illustrated by Bernard Long

© 1984 Rourke Enterprises, Inc.

Copyright © 1984 Martspress Ltd., Nork Way
Banstead, Surrey, SM7 1PB.

Library of Congress Cataloging in Publication Data

Oliver, Rupert.
  Dimetrodon.

  Summary: Sleeping and hunting for meat keep Dimetrodon
busy in his prehistoric day.
  1. Dimetrodon—Juvenile literature.   [1. Dimetrodon.
2. Dinosaurs]   I. Long, Bernard, ill.   II. Title.
QE862.P3044   1984   567.9′2   84-17866
ISBN 0-86592-210-1

Rourke Enterprises, Inc.
Vero Beach, FL 32964

Rhamphorhynchus

Pteranodon

Pterodactyl

Ankylosaurus

Dimetrodon

Iguanodon

Tricondon

Dimetrodon

Archaeopteryx

Ichthyosaurus

Plesiosaurus

Deinonychus

Nothosaurus

A Petrolacosaurus hurried out on to a fallen log to warm himself in the sun. Through the leaves overhead, the early morning sun was shining. Petrolacosaurus had come to lie in the sun because it gave him energy.

Suddenly, Petrolacosaurus saw something move a short distance away. A leathery, sail like fin came in sight. The fin belonged to one of the largest and most dangerous hunters, the Dimetrodon. At once Petrolacosaurus dashed back into the dense undergrowth.

Dimetrodon moved so that the warming rays of the sun shone on his sail. It was good to feel the sun warming his body. Soon he would be warm enough to go in search of food. Dimetrodon was hungry and he wanted meat.

As the sun rose in the sky, its heat warmed
Dimetrodon until he felt able to start hunting.
Dimetrodon raised himself up on his powerful legs
and walked off through the forest. As he walked, his
feet slipped in the sticky mixture of mud and fallen
leaves. It was always damp near the great delta as it
often rained.

As Dimetrodon pushed his way through the plants he kept a careful watch for any signs of life. He saw a small Cacops come out of the undergrowth. Even a small animal like this would make a tasty meal for Dimetrodon. Dimetrodon did not attack it. He had attacked a Cacops before. That was when Dimetrodon had broken one of his teeth on the bony plates on Cacops' back. He did not want to break another tooth, so he let the Cacops go. Unseen by either of the two animals, a tiny Cardiocephalus watched from a muddy pool.

A loud scream echoed through the lush plants. An animal was in trouble. When an animal is hurt, it is easier to catch. Perhaps this meant an easy meal for Dimetrodon. With a burst of speed, Dimetrodon plodded toward the sound.

Edaphosaurus was usually far too big for Dimetrodon to catch. However, when it became exhausted in the mud, Edaphosaurus would make an easy meal. Dimetrodon decided to wait. All the time the sun was getting hotter. Insects appeared and soon the air was alive with buzzing flies, bugs and dragonflies.

The Edaphosaurus continued to struggle in the mud. Suddenly it pulled itself free and Dimetrodon changed his mind about attacking. Wading off through the shallows, Edaphosaurus continued the search for tasty shellfish. An Ophiderpeton slid out of the mud. It hurried away from the hungry Edaphosaurus, across the surface of the mud, before tunneling down again in search of water bugs.

Dimetrodon splashed along the edge of the smelly pond. The sun was high in the sky now. As Dimetrodon plodded along he noticed a new smell. It was the scent of fresh, clean water. Dimetrodon was thirsty. The new scent made him want to quench his thirst even more. Dimetrodon ran through the trees as fast as his legs would carry him.

Soon Dimetrodon was out of the forest. Ahead were the shores of a wide lake. The sudden appearance of the fierce meat eater frightened the lakeside creatures. They ran for cover. A pair of Cacops dashed along the shore. A Seymouria hurried into the shrubs to hide. Much larger animals, like Eryops, waddled off toward the water where they felt safer. Soon all was quiet and Dimetrodon walked down to the water's edge and drank the cool, clean refreshing water.

When Dimetrodon finished drinking, he
looked around. The heads of the few Eryops broke
the surface of the lake. Otherwise the only moving life
was the insects flying through the air.

The sun was now very hot. It was so hot that
Dimetrodon began to feel uncomfortable and tired.
He knew that he would have to find a shady place to
rest until the air became cooler. Dimetrodon walked
back to the edge of the forest and settled down under
a clump of tree ferns.

Dimetrodon dozed through the heat of the day, while the insects whirred back and forth and Eryops splashed in the lake searching for fish.

When the temperature began to drop, Dimetrodon stretched his legs. It would soon be cool enough for him to move about again. Just then a cool breeze blew off the lake. Dimetrodon moved around so that his sail like fin would catch the breeze and cool him more quickly.

Suddenly, Dimetrodon heard loud footsteps behind him. There was something large moving just out of sight in the undergrowth. Dimetrodon poked his head through the leaves and saw the familiar sight of a Diadectes. Diadectes looked hot and tired. It would not be able to run very fast.

With a hungry roar Dimetrodon ran through
the undergrowth after the reptile. It saw Dimetrodon
and began to run as fast as it could. The ground
shook as the two reptiles lumbered along over the
slippery, mud covered leaves. Then, ahead of
Diadectes, there was a shallow muddy pool.

In his panic, the heavy reptile jumped into the pool, spraying mud and water everywhere. An animal, which had been feeding in the pool, scrambled out of the way as Dimetrodon charged in after the Diadectes.

The Diadectes tried to struggle through the mud to the far side of the pool but his legs became stuck in the mud and he did not have enough strength to pull them free. Swiftly the deadly jaws of Dimetrodon closed round the throat of Diadectes and the reptile breathed no more.

Without moving from the pond, Dimetrodon
tore at the carcass of Diadectes. With his strong
teeth, Dimetrodon tore great chunks of meat from the
body. He gulped them down without even chewing.

It was a long time before Dimetrodon had
satisfied his hunger. Finally, Dimetrodon crawled to
the edge of the pool and lay down to rest. The air was
growing chilly as the sun went down. Dimetrodon
found a place to lie down for the night. He would not
need to hunt again for several days.

Dimetrodon and Permian North America

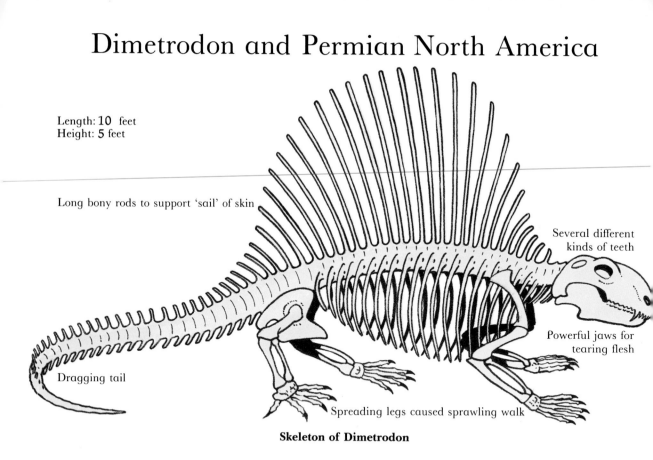

Length: **10** feet
Height: **5** feet

Long bony rods to support 'sail' of skin

Several different kinds of teeth

Dragging tail

Powerful jaws for tearing flesh

Spreading legs caused sprawling walk

Skeleton of Dimetrodon

When did Dimetrodon live?

Life has existed on the planet Earth for hundreds of millions of years, perhaps even three and a half thousand million years. Scientists have divided this immense period of time into four main sections. The earliest were the Azoic and Proterozoic. These lasted from the earliest times until 600 million years ago and there was little life at this time. The second era is known as the Paleozoic, which means 'ancient life'. This era saw the rise of animal and plant life, most of which was in water. The third era began about 225 million years ago and is called the Mesozoic, or 'middle life' when living things managed to colonize the land very successfully and is marked by the ascendency of mammals and birds. The fourth era, our own, is called Cenozoic, 'recent life'. It began about 65 million years ago. Dimetrodon lived about 260 million years ago. This means that it lived at the end of the Paleozoic era. Scientists have divided each era into a number of periods based on changing life forms. The final period of the Paleozoic era was the Permian. It was during this period that Dimetrodon lived and hunted.

Where did Dimetrodon live?

The fossils of Dimetrodon and the other animals Dimetrodon encounters in the story were all found in Texas. However, in the far distant days of the Permian period, Texas was not a hot dry state at all. As can be seen in the story it was the site of a large, marshy delta. This was the mouth of a large river which flowed into a small sea whose shores ran along the Texas-New Mexico border.

The life of a Dimetrodon

Dimetrodon was a large, meat-eating reptile which measured some ten feet from nose to tail. In common with all other reptiles it was cold-blooded. This could have been a great problem. No animal can be very active unless it is warm first and cold-blooded animals rely on the heat of the sun or air to warm them up. During the night, reptiles lose most of their heat. A reptile as large as Dimetrodon would have taken nearly three hours to warm up. This was the reason for the large 'sail' on Dimetrodon's back. By turning the sail to face the sun Dimetrodon was able to warm up much more quickly, perhaps in less than an hour. This helped Dimetrodon to spend a lot more time hunting. On the other hand, a reptile cannot remain active if it is too hot. By turning its 'sail' into a wind or by sitting in the shade Dimetrodon could cool down and remain active better than other reptiles. This was why Dimetrodon was able to catch Diadectes. The smaller reptile was still sluggish because it had not cooled down after the mid-day heat. Edaphosaurus would have used its sail in a similar way.

Permian amphibians and reptiles

The Permian period was a time when amphibians and reptiles were both important groups of land animals. The reptiles, such as Dimetrodon, were relatively new but the amphibians had been around for almost a hundred million years and were highly successful.

The amphibians of Permian Texas included Cacops, Cardiocephalus, Ophiderpeton, Seymouria, Eryops and Diplocaulus. Of these the six foot long Eryops was by far the largest. It was one of the biggest amphibians ever. Nearly all of these Permian amphibians were doomed to extinction. Only Cardiocephalus, or a close relative, survived and evolved into today's salamanders, frogs and toads.

Diadectes may also have been an amphibian.

The amphibians were driven into extinction by changing earth conditions and were replaced by the reptiles which were to rule the earth for the next 200 million years. Reptiles of the time included Dimetrodon, Edaphosaurus, Petrolacosaurus and, perhaps, Diadectes. Dimetrodon and Edaphosaurus survived for many years, but then died out. A related group of reptiles, the therapsids, followed these two giants and eventually evolved into the mammals. The small,

and insignificant, Petrolacosaurus managed to survive and evolve. Some sixty million years later the descendants of this reptile evolved into crocodiles, dinosaurs and, later still, into birds. It is easy to understand, therefore, that Petrolacosaurus was a very important reptile.

Why the reptiles took over

We have seen that during the early Permian, when Dimetrodon lived, there were as many, if not more, amphibians than reptiles. By the close of the period, the reptiles were far more important and the amphibians became very rare indeed. How did this happen?

Perhaps the answer lies with the egg. Amphibians lay small, soft eggs in water. It follows that young amphibians hatch when they are under-developed and have to spend the first part of their lives in the water. The eggs of the reptile are different.

As can be seen in the illustration below, the egg of a reptile has a tough shell and a yolk, or food store. The reptile egg with its hard, protective shell can be laid on land. This means that the young do not have to go through a water-living stage. Instead they emerge as miniature adults, ready and eager to start eating at once. It was probably this advantage and the fact that the dry land, well away from water, was available to them as living space that finally ensured the reptiles an important place in the world.

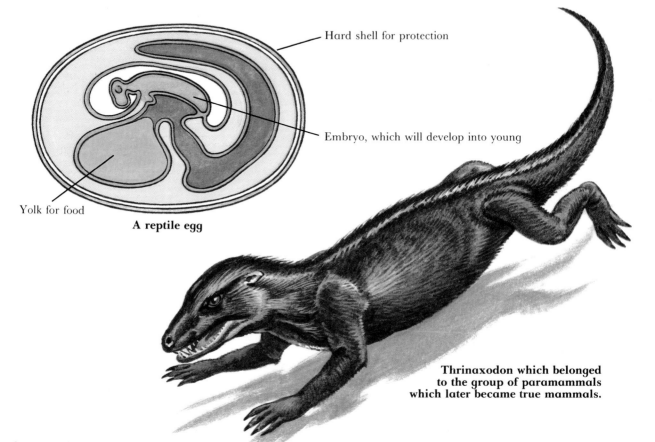

Hard shell for protection

Embryo, which will develop into young

Yolk for food

A reptile egg

Thrinaxodon which belonged to the group of paramammals which later became true mammals.